LOUIS VUITTON

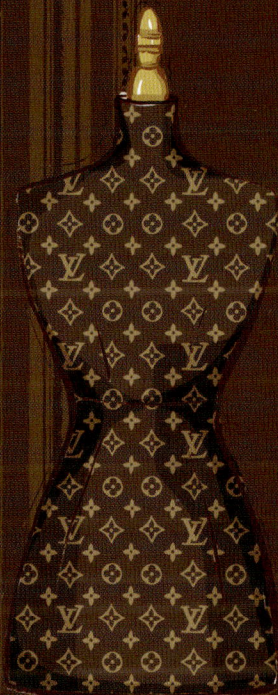

LOUIS VUITTON

For Neville John Hume,
my grandfather,

who could make and create anything
and encouraged me to do the same.

LOUIS VUITTON

THE ILLUSTRATED WORLD OF A FASHION ICON

Megan Hess

Hardie Grant

BOOKS

CONTENTS

INTRODUCTION

LV: two letters recognised the world over as a mark of travelling in style. Louis Vuitton revolutionised the art of luggage during the dawn of the modern travel era in the mid-1800s. In doing so, he laid the foundations of an unparalleled legacy in fashion.

IN 1854, after many years of learning the highly skilled trade of trunkmaking and packing, Louis Vuitton had the vision to start his own maison. He had already risen to the top of his trade in Paris, being personally chosen by the French empress – along with the rest of the country's fashionable elite – to build custom trunks in which to carefully pack the beautiful gowns that they ferried between palaces and cities across Europe.

But Louis Vuitton knew there was more on his horizon. Louis, and his son and grandson after him, pioneered innovations to luggage, at a time when trains, ships, cars and planes were making travel easier. Their lightweight trunks in beautiful, patterned fabrics became must-have travel items, not just for Parisians but for the members of the elite living in every glamorous city across the world, including maharajas and movie stars.

This multi-generational business saw the possibilities in making luggage that was practical but also elegant and in designing; luggage that was custom-made to house everything from opera costumes to explorers' equipment. It is no surprise that the maison's subsequent forays into handbags and clothing would continue to build upon that. The distinctive Louis Vuitton Monogram signals quality and style in every sense, and Louis Vuitton eventually grew into one of the biggest fashion houses in the world.

The breathtaking success of Louis Vuitton is all the more incredible when you learn that the man himself built it from scratch. He left his difficult rural home as a boy and made the long journey to Paris to experience something new, seek his fortune and perhaps leave his mark on the world. He could surely not have imagined quite how much of a mark that would be.

Louis Vuitton's bravery and perseverance, as well as his commitment to creating beautiful and practical objects, have meant that his name and his story will forevermore be connected to luxury and adventure.

1

THE
MAN

IT FEELS APPROPRIATE that the story of Louis Vuitton starts with a journey. But this isn't an opulent voyage – at least, not yet. In fact, it's a journey of a boy who sets out from his home in a French farming village to cross the country, on foot. Despite his humble beginnings, he had big dreams, and he was ready to follow them.

Louis Vuitton arrived in Paris on the edge of the Industrial Revolution. The bustling city must have felt a world away from village life. His practical skills quickly earnt him an apprenticeship as a trunkmaker and packer, a fateful choice that would eventually see him work for the most famous and fashionable names in France, most notably Empress Eugénie de Montijo.

While his skills made him a master of his craft, Louis also had the ability to think outside the box, and his innovations helped him create one of the world's most significant brands, established decades ahead of most of today's celebrated fashion houses. While Louis Vuitton's early life is not well documented, the details that we do know form a portrait of a truly extraordinary man.

Louis Vuitton was born on 4 August 1821
in a quiet rural village called Anchay.
His parents, Xavier and Coronne,
had a small farm.

Coronne was also a milliner, making hats
that perhaps inspired a young Louis to
be interested in style.

Louis spent his childhood helping with jobs
so that the family could make ends meet.

Anchay was little more than a few cottages and farms in the shadow of the Jura Mountains in France's east, where the snowy winters could be particularly hard.

It was the kind of place that most people only left to visit the neighbouring village, and Louis's family had lived there for generations.

Louis's mother died when
he was just ten years old.

The struggles and monotony of rural life
suddenly felt even more difficult, especially
after his father remarried and Louis clashed
with his strict new stepmother.

Louis took solace in his affinity for making
things with wood from the nearby forest.
But he wished for something more.

So at the age of just thirteen, Louis waited
for the winter snow to melt, then set out alone
on the journey that would change his life.

The road from Anchay to Paris is
more than 400 kilometres. As he had
no money, Louis had no option but
to walk the whole way there.

It took him more than two years.

Louis stopped along the route to do odd jobs in exchange for food and shelter – helping on farms like the one he had grown up on or sometimes, assisting craftspeople.

With his love of making, he quickly developed skills in several trades.

Carriages laden with trunks would have likely passed Louis on the road as they journeyed to far-off places.

Perhaps that romantic sight sparked an
idea for the young traveller, which helped
motivate him on his long journey.

"

I always find
BEAUTY IN THINGS
that are odd
AND IMPERFECT –
they are much more
INTERESTING.

"

MARC JACOBS

LOUIS VUITTON

It was 1837 when Louis arrived in Paris. He was now sixteen years old. This was the eve of the Industrial Revolution, and Paris was a centre of commerce and culture.

The lively streets would have been quite an experience compared to the quiet, rural landscapes that Louis was used to.

But the city was also a difficult place, and if Louis was going to survive there – let alone make his mark – then he was going to need an occupation.

Luckily, young Louis's skills as a maker
were quickly recognised by another
skilful maker, Romain Maréchal.

Monsieur Maréchal was a famous
malletier et emballeur (trunkmaker and
packer) and Louis proved himself worthy
of an apprenticeship for this traditional
and highly respected craft.

This happened to be an exciting new era for travel. The first railroad into Paris opened the same year that Louis arrived in the city.

Wealthy and adventurous citizens
were beginning to take journeys across
the ocean on steamboats (themselves
a French invention).

Travel wasn't usually just a matter
of days or weeks – people would
spend months or years travelling.

As they would be away for such
a long time, travellers needed
to carry a lot of items with them.
And those items needed to be
carefully packed in bespoke
trunks and boxes.

At Monsieur Maréchal's workshop on the stylish
Rue Saint-Honoré, Louis went from sweeping the
workshop floor to helping the master craftsmen,
learning how to fashion beautiful custom travel
boxes from top-quality wood and leather.
He spent seventeen years perfecting the craft.

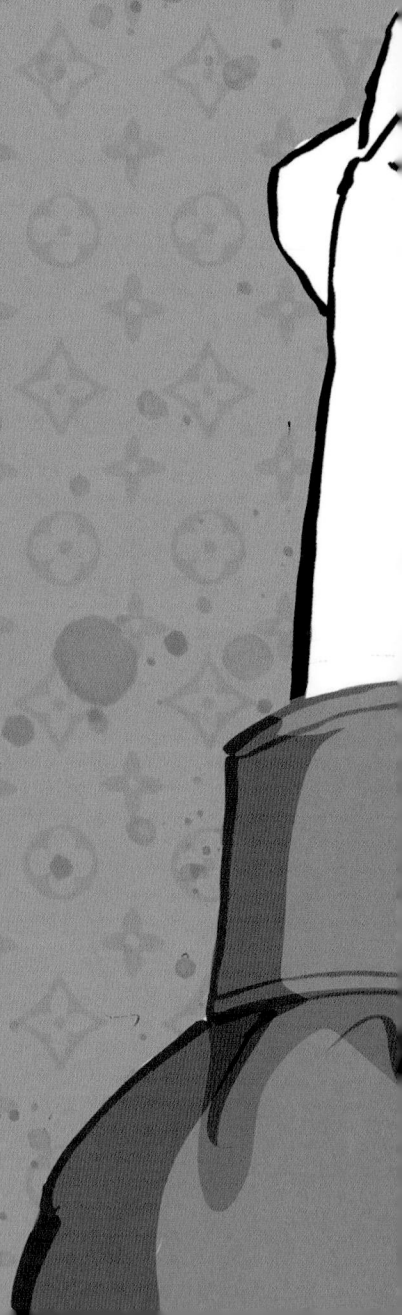

Part of the service of a malletier et emballeur
was not just to make the trunks but also
to pack their precious contents to ensure
everything arrived safe and sound.

This included packing the delicate and
extravagant outfits that important clients
would require for long journeys.

And when it came to packing fashion,
Louis Vuitton earnt a reputation for
being the best of the best.

Now a master craftsman himself, Louis was
in demand among the nobility of France.

But the highest honour came
when he was personally selected
to be the malletier et emballeur for
Eugénie de Montijo, the wife of
France's new emperor, Napoleon III.

Louis was entrusted to design and create her
bespoke trunks, then pack them with the
exquisite gowns befitting the empress's
opulent lifestyle, as she travelled from the
Tuileries Palace in Paris to her country
escape at the Château de Saint-Cloud
and across the rest of the country and
overseas as part of her official duties.

Spanish-born Empress Eugénie used fashion to signal her status as well as her style. She was a great supporter of the burgeoning couture industry that was just starting up in Paris.

She famously changed outfits multiple times a day and had great influence across France and the world, as admirers rushed to emulate her iconic looks.

Empress Eugénie was a patron
of the English-born couture pioneer
Charles Frederick Worth, who
created lavish one-of-a-kind dresses
as the House of Worth.

Louis Vuitton befriended his fellow
creator as they worked together to keep
the empress well-dressed in all moments
and places. During this time, Louis
developed a deeper appreciation for the
art of fashion.

HOUSE OF WORTH

The year 1854 was a very important one for Louis Vuitton. First, he married Clemence-Emilie Parriaux, the young daughter of a mill owner.

Then, with some extra encouragement and assistance from his new wife, Louis opened his own eponymous atelier.

His success thus far had given him confidence and credibility, and he had grand ideas to improve on the historic craft of trunkmaking and packing, particularly for the fashionable set.

The first Louis Vuitton atelier was
at 4 Rue Neuve-des-Capucines.

It was a wealthy area in the heart of Paris,
close to the regal Place Vendôme and to many
couturiers, including Monsieur Maréchal's
workshop and the House of Worth.

The building housed a small workshop
downstairs, and the newly wed Louis
and Clemence-Emilie lived above it.

The sign in the window read:
'Securely packs the most fragile objects.
Specialising in packing fashion.'

"

NEVER FORGET
that what becomes
TIMELESS WAS
once truly new.

"

NICOLAS GHESQUIÈRE

Inspired by the progress of the Industrial
Revolution, Louis started exploring the
use of advanced materials, including zinc,
aluminium and copper, to create trunks that
were more durable and lightweight.

Louis's experiments led to
his first major innovation in
luggage design.

In 1858, Louis Vuitton introduced
the flat-topped steamer trunk.

Trunks had previously been made with a
domed lid so that any rain would roll off and
not damage the leather if the luggage was
exposed to the elements in transit.

But Louis's new trunk was made from a
canvas that he called Trianon – perhaps
named for the beautiful countryside
villas that his clients visited.

Trianon canvas, in addition to being
more hardwearing than leather,
was waterproof, meaning that the
trunks could have a flat top.

This had the very important benefit
of allowing the trunks to be stacked,
which was especially useful for the
newly popular train and ship travel.

Of course, as well as being practical, Louis Vuitton's new trunks were beautiful. The Trianon canvas looked elegant and modern.

Empress Eugénie was an early adopter, and very soon Louis's steamer trunks became the must-have travel accessory.

Demand grew rapidly, and the Vuitton family was also about to expand.

It was clear that they would need more space than their Parisian shopfront and apartment could offer.

Louis decided to look beyond the crowded city and settled on a plot of land in Asnières-sur-Seine, in the countryside just outside of Paris.

There he set about building a state-of-the-art, light-filled workshop from glass and steel, fitting of an innovative business.

The location on the River Seine easily allowed Louis to import the premium materials he needed for his trunks, and to send the trunks off to be sold at his Paris shopfront.

Louis Vuitton also designed and built a family home
next door to his workshop in Asnières-sur-Seine.

Complete with detailed stained-glass windows,
a well-stocked library and antique furnishings, this house
reflected the impeccable taste that Louis had developed
through his work with Paris's most stylish clientele.

It was a long way from
the humble farmhouse
of his childhood.

It was the ideal home in
which to welcome a new member
of the Vuitton family.

Louis and Clemence-Emilie
celebrated the birth of their son,
Georges, in 1857.

With his new workshop busier than ever
and his wife and son settled in their beautiful
home, all the foundations were set for
Louis Vuitton to become the most important
luggage maker in France, and very soon,
the world.

2

THE
BRAND

THE TRANSITION OF LOUIS VUITTON into the label we know today was not without bumps in the road. But it should come as no surprise, after his remarkable beginnings, that Louis Vuitton had the resilience to work through these difficulties in order to take his luggage to every corner of the globe, creating custom trunks for everyone from explorers to opera stars.

By the time he passed away in the late 1800s, Louis Vuitton had trained his son, Georges, to continue the business in the same spirit of boundless ideas. Georges then passed the baton to his own son, Gaston-Louis. Over the generations, the Vuitton family never stopped finding ways to innovate, from the unpickable lock to the travel-ready car trunk and, of course, the iconic Monogram pattern.

None other than Coco Chanel would have a hand in Louis Vuitton's expansion into handbags in the early twentieth century. From there, the brand was unstoppable, making beautiful pieces of all shapes and sizes. A Louis Vuitton bag was truly the ideal accessory, not just for travel, but for anyone on the go.

In 1867, Paris hosted the Exposition Universelle: an enormous fair with more than 50 000 stalls displaying the best products and ideas from across the world.

And Louis Vuitton was indisputably the best when it came to luggage.

With six million visitors travelling to the exposition, Louis had a chance to expand his clientele beyond Paris.

His stall was the talk of the grand event, and he was even awarded the fair's bronze medal for his efforts.

LOUIS VUITTON

But Louis Vuitton's luck
was about to change.

In 1870, the Franco-Prussian War
and the start of the resulting Siege of
Paris saw demand for luxury goods
drop rapidly and the once-busy
streets emptied.

Louis Vuitton's most important
client, Empress Eugénie, went
into exile with her husband.

The Louis Vuitton workshop
was looted and destroyed and
the Paris shop had to close.

Louis Vuitton, resourceful as ever,
organised rationing supplies to help with
food shortages and offered his stock
of materials for useful purposes.

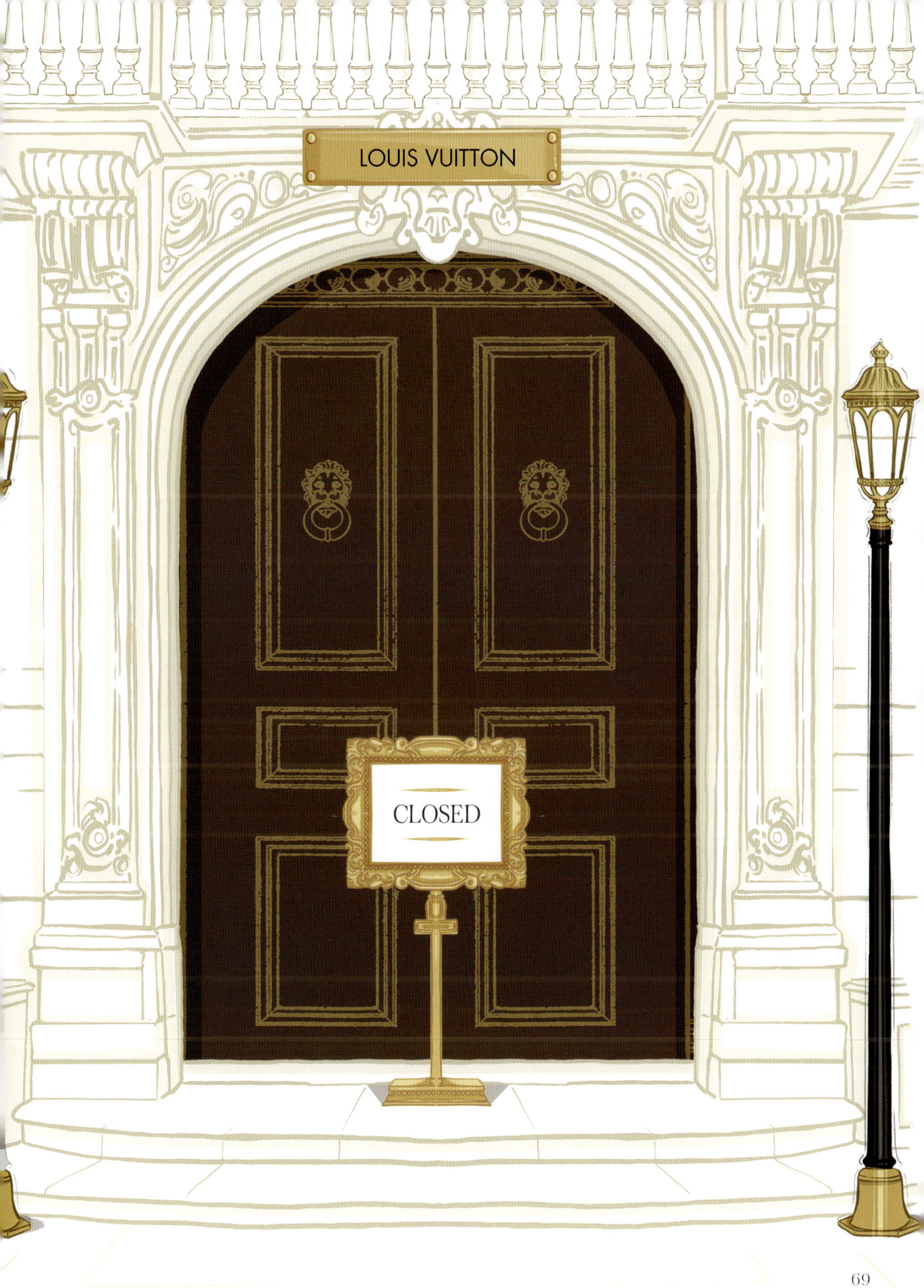
LOUIS VUITTON
CLOSED

Once the city opened again, Louis was characteristically determined not just to rebuild but to expand the business.

He took the opportunity to create a bigger and better workshop, and to open a new store in Paris.

The second Louis Vuitton shopfront
opened in 1871 at 1 Rue Scribe, surrounded
by boutiques and close to the opera house
and the stately Grand Hôtel.

It was the perfect spot to start a new era
for the maison.

A year later, Louis Vuitton expanded his line
by introducing the striped Rayée canvas.

The canvas was available in red and brown
variations, and marked another leap in the
possibilities of travelling in style.

It also began a Louis Vuitton trademark of
creating distinctive patterns that made its
quality goods immediately recognisable.

This put Louis Vuitton a step ahead of its
competitors, who were eager to reproduce
Louis Vuitton's popular creations.

Louis hoped his son, Georges,
would take over the family business.

Louis's own difficult childhood made
him determined to give Georges the
education that he never had himself.

In fact, Louis and Clemence-Emilie
decided to send Georges to study on
the British island of Jersey so that Georges
could get an excellent education and learn
to speak English fluently.

LOU

This would allow Georges to communicate
easily with the brand's new global clientele.

In 1882, Clemence-Emilie passed away. Louis was in his sixties, and the future of the business was very much on his mind.

Georges, who had spent his younger years in and around workshops, was now ready to learn the art of trunkmaking beside his father.

Luckily, Georges was an enthusiastic apprentice with an even bigger vision for the work his father had started.

In 1885, Georges was sent to London
to open the first Louis Vuitton
shop outside of France.

The store, on Oxford Street, marked both
a key moment in the expansion of the Louis
Vuitton name and in Georges's growing
role in the business.

The 'French trunk' store, as it became
known, eventually moved to the upmarket
shopping area of New Bond Street.

Louis Vuitton was now making trunks
for important clients all over the world,
customised to their exact needs.

This included everything from a bed trunk
for explorers seeking the best in innovative
travel goods, to the celebrated wardrobe
trunk (Malle Chemise) with drawers,
which allowed fashionable travellers the
convenience of not needing to unpack
their bags on their journey.

In 1889, over two decades after the last Exposition Universelle, Paris hosted another world fair, and Louis Vuitton was there again to share his travel wares with the world.

This time he won a gold medal.

The 1889 world fair saw the unveiling of an iconic engineering feat that dominated the Paris skyline: the Eiffel Tower.

Also featuring at the 1889 world fair
was a new pattern for Louis Vuitton:
the Damier (or checkerboard) canvas.

Originally available in brown (Ebène) and now also known for its blue (Azur) variation, it remains an iconic symbol of the brand.

Louis Vuitton himself could now also lay claim to being an icon.

He had built a growing empire on the back of his skills and vision, and his trunks were the epitome of luxury travel.

Louis died at home in Asnières-sur-Seine in 1892 at the age of seventy.

He was buried in the
local cemetery alongside
Clemence-Emilie.

"

Show me YOUR LUGGAGE and I'll tell you WHO YOU ARE.

"

LOUIS VUITTON ADVERTISING
CAMPAIGN SLOGAN, 1921

Louis had ensured the continuation
of his maison through his son.

Georges demonstrated that he truly followed
in his father's footsteps when he introduced
the second major Louis Vuitton innovation in
the form of the 'unpickable' tumbler lock.

The lock, which was officially launched
in 1890, allowed travellers to feel
confident that their precious cargo
was safe in a Louis Vuitton trunk.

Georges even challenged Harry Houdini
to try to unpick the lock.

Houdini didn't take up the challenge,
perhaps because the locks were so
famously impenetrable.

In 1893 there was another world fair,
this time held in Chicago.

After his father's success at world
fairs, Georges saw an opportunity
to introduce Louis Vuitton to the
booming American market.
It was an instant triumph.

Georges sold all the goods he had
brought over for the event, and he
soon opened Louis Vuitton stores
in Washington and New York,
with more to come.

Georges also continued the
Louis Vuitton tradition of distinctive
patterns, and none had more impact
than the Louis Vuitton Monogram.

The unmistakable design is made
of three floral shapes and the
interlaced LV initials.

Georges introduced the
Monogram in 1896 as a wonderful
tribute to his father.

The Monogram pattern drew on a range of artistic influences, including a rosette or quatrefoil motif on a medieval box that may have been among Louis Vuitton's antique collection.

It also references the Japanese Mon
designs that were fashionable in Europe
during the Victorian era.

The name Louis Vuitton continued to
be inextricably tied to the revolution in
glamorous travel. Georges particularly loved
automobiles, and designed specific trunks
to fit with new car models.

A road trunk was the ideal way to pack for
an escape to the picturesque Côte d'Azur,
which was incidentally where Georges
opened the next Louis Vuitton store in 1908.

There were Louis Vuitton
trunks designed to fit in hot air
balloons and aeroplanes.

Louis Vuitton even exhibited a prototype helicopter
at the 1910 Paris art and technology exposition.
It was designed by Georges's twenty-year-old twins
Jean and Pierre Vuitton – two of Georges's five
children with his wife, Joséphine.

Sadly, Jean Vuitton died three days
before the show opened.

People travelled with their Louis Vuitton luggage by road, by air and by sea.

It was rumoured that Louis Vuitton trunks were the only luggage that survived the tragic sinking of the Titanic in 1912.

In 1913 the doors of a new Louis Vuitton store opened at 101 Champs-Élysées,
in an impressive seven-storey Art Deco building commissioned by Georges.

The store, which is still the Paris flagship and a landmark on the city's best-known boulevard, was recognised as the largest travel goods store in the world.

By the 1920s there were Louis Vuitton stores in major cities across the world.

From Bombay to Buenos Aires, the maison was renowned for the bespoke orders it fulfilled for special clientele, including an art trunk made for famous gallerist René Gimpel to carefully transport priceless paintings, and a desk trunk for writer Ernest Hemingway complete with spaces for his typewriter and book collection.

In 1905, French actor Sarah Bernhardt took a suite of 200 Louis Vuitton trunks with her on a tour of Brazil.

A dressing case designed for celebrated French opera singer Marthe Chenal included special compartments to store her cosmetic brushes and compacts.

And a trunk made for another star of the stage, Lily Pons, had space to carry twenty-six glamorous pairs of shoes across the world.

On the other side of the Atlantic, fashionable icons of the silver screen such as Greta Garbo, Katharine Hepburn and Elizabeth Taylor were all known for carrying Louis Vuitton luggage whenever they travelled for work or play.

"

LOUIS VUITTON
is about travel,
CREATIVITY,
and innovation.

"

NICOLAS GHESQUIÈRE

Louis Vuitton picnic trunks, polo trunks and fishing trunks were made for sultans, maharajas and emperors.

In 1938 the company made special trunks lined with pink moiré silk to house a pair of dolls for English princesses Elizabeth and Margaret, to commemorate their visit to Paris with King George VI.

Georges Vuitton was particularly passionate about making all Louis Vuitton customers feel special.

For particularly loyal patrons, he designed a mini version of the classic trunk that would be delivered with a bunch of flowers inside.

There was another mini design that would
mark a major shift in the Louis Vuitton story.

The brand had marked the start of
the twentieth century by introducing
a soft-sided bag.

The Steamer was designed to be kept
inside a trunk as a way of separating clean
and worn linen on an ocean voyage.

But in true Louis Vuitton style, these bags
were as glamorous as they were functional.

So perhaps it's no surprise that they caught the eye of a fashion legend.

In 1915, who else but Coco Chanel requested Louis Vuitton to make her a personalised version of the Steamer.

It featured a structured domed silhouette with a double-zipper closure and a padlock, and was a perfect size to carry throughout the day.

In the 1930s, Coco Chanel gave permission for a version of the bag (with her characteristic CC replaced with an LV) to be released for sale as the Squire. It was renamed in 1992 as the Alma, after the Place de l'Alma in Paris.

The 1930s was an era when women were gaining independence, and the handbag became a symbol of that.

These bags were not just beautifully crafted pieces that could be matched to the wearer's outfit, but also practical companions for years to come.

That mix of beauty and useability remains
characteristic of a Louis Vuitton bag.

There is another classic Louis Vuitton
bag with an iconic woman behind it.

The Express was originally introduced
in 1930, with its name reflecting the
dizzying pace of modern travel.

But in 1965 Audrey Hepburn requested
a smaller version to add to her timeless
wardrobe, and this became the Speedy.

Hepburn carried the bag with
her across the world, always
looking incredibly chic.

The 1930s was a prolific period for Louis Vuitton bag designs, with the Keepall and the Noé also released at that time.

As the name suggests, the Keepall was designed as a large duffle fit for a spontaneous weekend getaway.

Featuring straps and laced sides that could be adjusted for size and comfort, it was a favourite of Brigitte Bardot.

The Noé bucket bag was originally designed to carry bottles of the best French champagne.

The designer of both of these classics was Georges's eldest son, Gaston-Louis Vuitton. Georges was now planning his own legacy.

Of his five children, two had died in infancy and one of the twins, Jean, had died in 1910.

The surviving twin, Pierre, was fatally wounded while serving as a pilot in World War I, which itself marked a difficult time for the business in many ways.

Fortunately, Gaston-Louis was ready to carry on the Louis Vuitton name.

Born in 1883, Gaston-Louis Vuitton was a man of many creative interests, as well as a skilled artisan and salesperson like his father and grandfather.

Georges continued to expand his vision for
what Louis Vuitton could offer the world,
with the help of Gaston-Louis.

At the 1925 Paris Exposition Internationale of
modern and decorative arts – a touchstone
of the Art Deco movement – the brand
exhibited not just luggage but furniture,
glassware and ceramics made in collaboration
with skilled artisans.

LOUIS VUITTON

LOUIS VUITTON

LOUIS VUITTON

The collaboration was particularly
fitting considering Louis Vuitton's own
experience working alongside a range
of craftspeople during his youth.

LOUIS VUITTON

FURNITURE

LOUIS VUITTON

Apart from a Louis Vuitton purse or wallet, what
better to pack in your Louis Vuitton suitcase than a
Louis Vuitton book? Georges penned a history of travel,
Le Voyage, in 1894, which highlighted the various types of
luggage people had carried with them on journeys throughout
the centuries. The brand's series of books is still expanding today,
including beautiful artist publications and city guidebooks.

Louis Vuitton released
its first scent, Heures
d'Absence, in 1927.

Of course, travel was the
inspiration – the bottle was
shaped like a roadside marker
and engraved with an aeroplane.

Only 300 bottles were
made of the first edition
of this scent.

The scent was named after the Vuittons' new country retreat – a mark that the family had now joined the echelons of society that a young Louis Vuitton had once learnt to make trunks for.

Georges Vuitton died in Asnières-sur-Seine in 1936 at the age of seventy-nine. He had seen his father's company through an astounding period of global expansion, and now left it in the hands of Gaston-Louis Vuitton.

The industry and the family were
about to enter a difficult period during
World War II, but the end of the war
saw a new demand for French luxury
goods, including Louis Vuitton
bags – a firm favourite of the much-
photographed, jet-setting fashion set.

Gaston-Louis was particularly
recognised for his fantastical window
displays, which changed weekly at
the Champs-Élysées store, and
were based on his sketches.

This commitment to wonderful
windows is a tradition that the
brand has very much continued.

LOUIS VUITTON

139

Gaston-Louis was also
an avid collector.

His vast and curious collections
included trunks, of course, as well as locks
and other travel items, art from across the
world, toys and even walking sticks.

He also collected thousands of whimsical
postcards and vintage travel stickers, the
kind that would've been stuck all over Louis
Vuitton trunks in an earlier era of travel.

The brand's designers still use
items from Gaston-Louis's
archive for inspiration.

LOUIS
VUITTON

27.02.1892

Gaston-Louis Vuitton ran Louis Vuitton with the help
of his own sons until his death in 1970, marking three
generations of the Vuitton family running the business.

GEORGES
VUITTON

26.10.1936

GASTON-LOUIS
VUITTON

17.03.1970

By this time, Louis Vuitton had not only become
synonymous with travelling trunks, but it laid claim
to producing the most fashionable bags for all occasions.

3

THE
LEGEND

OVER THE YEARS, Louis Vuitton has continued to expand across the world, with luggage, handbags and leather goods still the brand's core offering.

After over 100 years of family ownership, the business merged with another French luxury brand, the champagne house Moët Hennessy, to become LVMH in 1987.

A new era was still to come, one that expanded on Louis Vuitton's legacy of style. The original Louis Vuitton trunks had been specially made for packing beautiful clothes, but Louis Vuitton was now about to make its own beautiful clothes. A designer by the name of Marc Jacobs would quickly solidify Louis Vuitton as one of the top fashion houses, making the brand a cult favourite among stars of a new generation.

Louis Vuitton has continued to evolve in a way that honours the brand's historic beginnings, but also looks to the future with an emphasis on technology and sustainability.
And a sense of adventure is still at the heart of it all.

In 1996, Louis Vuitton marked the centenary of perhaps its
most recognised design feature: the iconic Monogram pattern
that Georges Vuitton had created to honour his father.

It was celebrated in a distinctively Louis Vuitton manner, by
collaborating with a number of top fashion designers. The coveted
collection included pieces from Azzedine Alaïa, Manolo Blahnik and
Vivienne Westwood. Its success might have also sparked a new idea.

The next year saw a major turning point for Louis Vuitton, when a bold, young American designer was brought on as creative director and charged with designing the brand's first ready-to-wear line of clothing.

For his debut Louis Vuitton collection, Marc Jacobs created luxurious but relaxed travel-appropriate clothes.

Handbags and the Monogram were conspicuously absent from this line, but Jacobs wanted to push the boundaries for Louis Vuitton, while still taking inspiration from the grey Trianon trunks for which the maison was first known.

Marc Jacobs succeeded in quickly establishing Louis Vuitton as a fully-fledged fashion house, with more wearable offerings honouring the magic of travel at every step.

Jacobs' first jewellery collection for Louis Vuitton included a charm bracelet adorned with the kinds of trinkets one might collect across global adventures, including a mini Eiffel Tower, aeroplane and suitcase.

Jacobs revitalised the historic Louis Vuitton brand with his quirky counterculture aesthetic and pop-culture connections.

Celebrities like David Bowie, Madonna and Nicole Kidman began appearing in Louis Vuitton campaigns and wearing Louis Vuitton clothes on the runway and the red carpet.

Jacobs also continued the brand's commitment to creative collaboration, most notably with American artist Stephen Sprouse and Japanese artist Takashi Murakami.

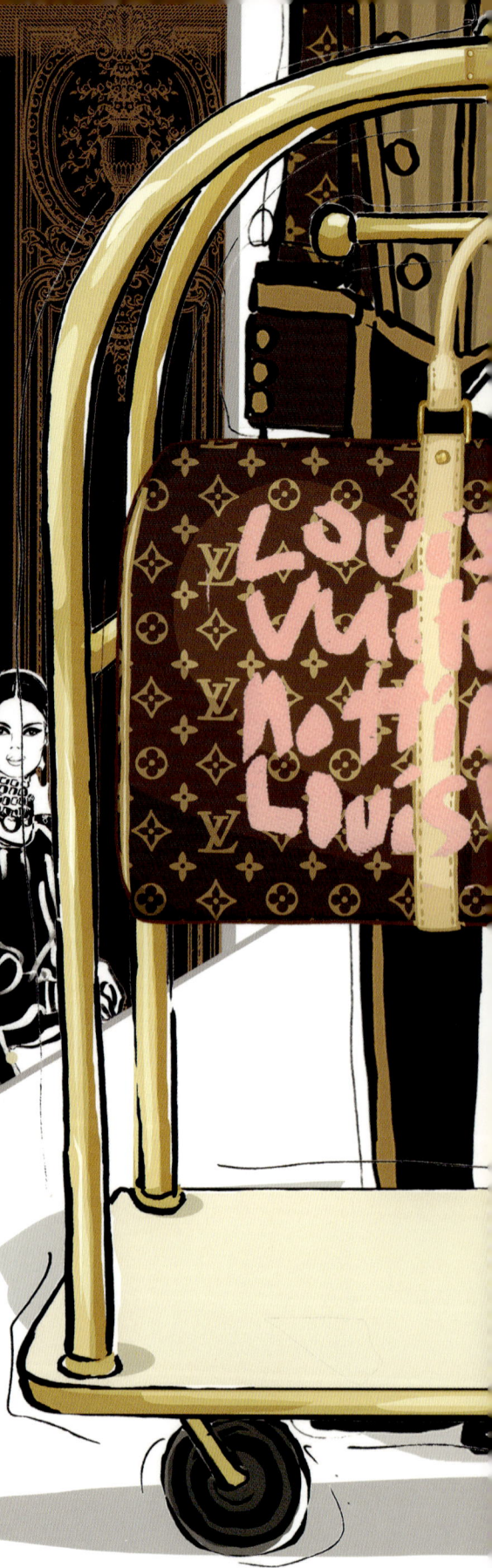

Sprouse's neon graffiti take on the Louis Vuitton logo caused a stir when it appeared in 2001 on bags carried down the runway by luggage porters.

And Murakami's candy-coloured version of the Monogram was a surprisingly popular diversion from the classic chocolate-and-tan variation.

There was no doubt that Louis Vuitton had entered an exciting new era.

Under Marc Jacobs's creative eye, Louis Vuitton runways were always a spectacle.

The 2010 show featured a show-stopping water fountain, while in 2011 Kate Moss appeared perched on a stunning Parisian carousel.

Things escalated again in 2012 with models in vintage looks walking beside a life-size Louis Vuitton train.

When it came time for Marc Jacobs to leave Louis Vuitton to focus on his own label in 2014, the set for his last runway show referenced all of these iconic moments, and was a perfect swan song for a designer who had changed Louis Vuitton forever.

French designer Nicolas Ghesquière took over as artistic director of Louis Vuitton in 2013, after designing at Balenciaga.

Known for his experimental, space-age influences, Ghesquière embraced a modern look for Louis Vuitton, fitting the brand's forward-thinking approach.

His architectural-inspired debut collection for Louis Vuitton was appropriately titled 'A new day'.

Louis Vuitton menswear was first introduced under Marc Jacobs in 2011 and has become a pillar of the brand's fashion line under the guidance of some high-profile heads.

Kim Jones introduced Louis Vuitton collaborations with streetwear brand Supreme, while Off-White designer Virgil Abloh brought a distinct playfulness and inclusivity to his tragically short time at the brand before his death from cancer at just forty-one.

MARC JACOBS

KIM JONES

Superstar singer Pharrell Williams has continued the street-style appeal and pop-culture collaborations, opening the brand to a new generation of fans.

VIRGIL ABLOH

PHARRELL WILLIAMS

"

I DON'T HAVE
to choose between
HIGH FASHION
or streetwear.

"

VIRGIL ABLOH

Louis Vuitton runways are often staged in incredible
travel destinations, such as Rio's cutting-edge Niterói
Contemporary Art Museum, the otherworldly,
Gaudí-designed Park Güell in Barcelona, and,
of course, the Musée de Louvre in Paris.

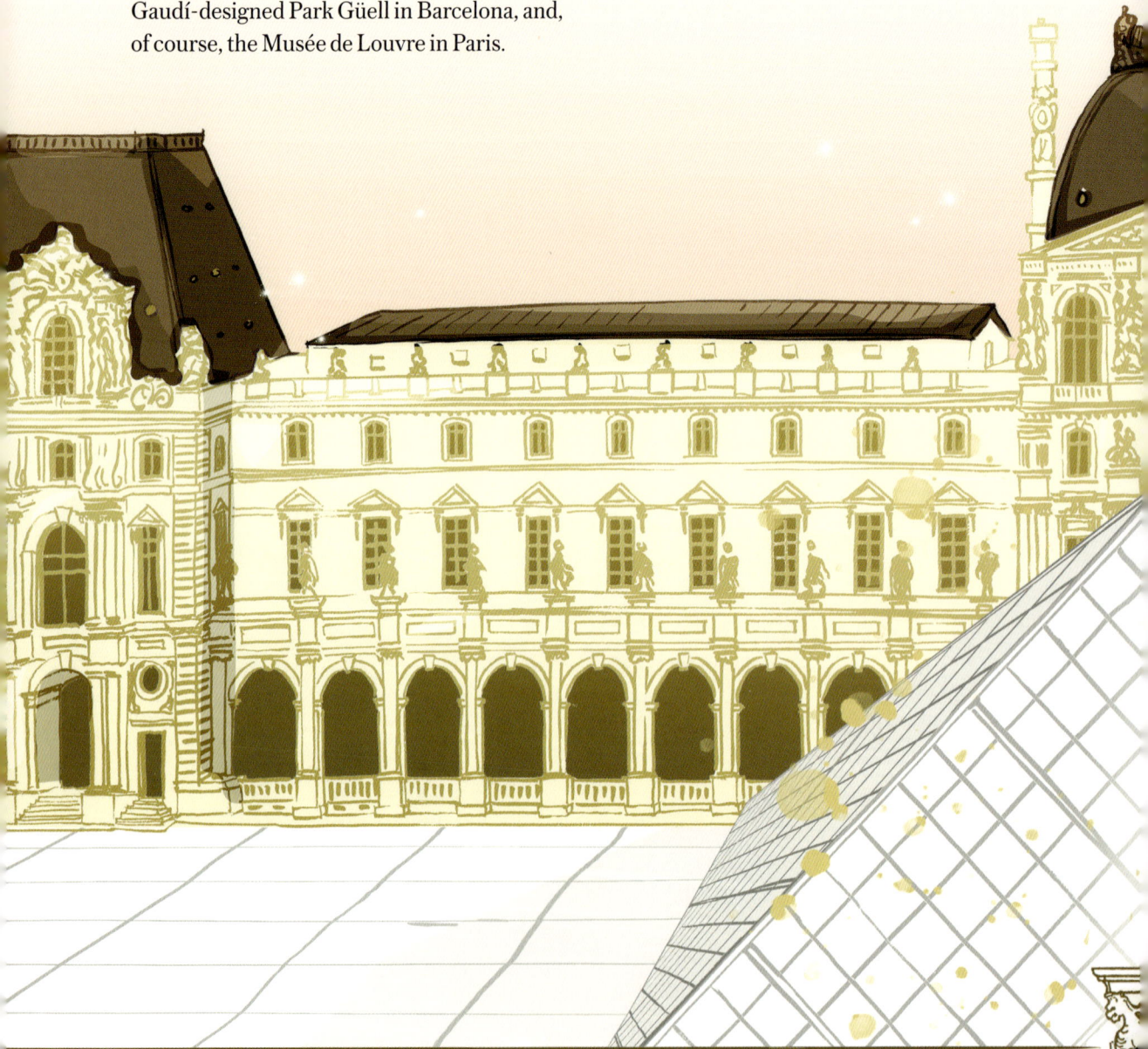

The company reuses or recycles the materials from its amazing runways and window displays.

LOUIS VUITTON

Bags are unsurprisingly still the most
celebrated Louis Vuitton pieces.

The brand's heritage designs are as loved by today's
fashion icons as they were in previous centuries.

Newer styles, such as the Monceau, the Papillon and the
Pochette Métis, are available in supple Epi leather, and in
Monogram denim or Econyl nylon, made from waste products.

The most popular Louis Vuitton bags
are often the products of collaborations,
including the signature spots of Japanese
artist Yayoi Kusama, and the cat sketches
of *Vogue* legend Grace Coddington.

In an apt connection to Coco's role in the
introduction of the Louis Vuitton handbag,
Chanel designer Karl Lagerfeld contributed
a design for the brand's 'The icon and the
iconoclasts' project in 2014.

Ghesquière's own covetable bag designs
reference Louis Vuitton's early days, including
the Capucines, named in honour of the brand's
first store on Rue Neuve-des-Capucines, and
the Petite Malle (or little trunk), a wearable
tribute to the original Louis Vuitton luggage.

The maison is still meticulously
hand-crafting custom trunks using designs
that remain largely unchanged from
Louis Vuitton's originals, with the mantra:
'No dream is too large or object too complex.'

Trunks have been made to house
record collections, watercolour paints,
skateboards, birthday cakes, trophies
for the French Open and medals for the
2024 Paris Olympic Games.

There is even a party trunk,
complete with champagne glasses
and a Monogram disco ball.

The brand honours its long and
eventful history while always finding
ways to look ahead.

It marked 200 years since Louis Vuitton's
birth by creating a virtual game to celebrate
the founder and his spirit, alongside a
book containing the visions and desires of
200 creative people from around the world.

LOU

LOUIS VUITTON

LOUIS VUITTON

LOUIS V

VUITTON

Louis Vuitton himself would be pleased
to know that innovative luggage is still
a key offering.

LOUIS VUITTON

LOUIS VUITTON

LOUIS VUI

LOUIS VUI ON

The incredibly lightweight Horizon and
Pégase suitcases were introduced in
collaboration with influential Australian
industrial designer Marc Newson.

They feature in luxury hotel lobbies
the world over.

One place that Louis Vuitton suitcases are sure to be seen is at the first Louis Vuitton hotel.

Built to replicate a huge Monogram trunk, it sits alongside the flagship store on the Champs-Élysées.

The brand has also opened a Paris store in Place Vendôme, just around the corner from the original Rue Neuve-des-Capucines store.

Like everything Louis Vuitton does, its buildings are designed as a testament to innovation and aesthetics.

There are now twenty-one Louis Vuitton ateliers throughout France, as well as workshops and stores across the world.

The original workshop in Asnières-sur-Seine is still dedicated to the bespoke orders on which the house was founded.

As well as the workshop, you can also visit the beautiful home that Louis Vuitton built for his family.

For spring–summer 2023, Nicolas Ghesquière designed an exquisite tribute in the form of the Maison de Famille, a handbag-sized trunk in the shape of the Vuitton family home.

It seems perfect that a brand founded on travel, by a boy who walked all the way to Paris to follow his dreams, has been honoured with its own address.

The workshop and home in Asnières-sur-Seine are now found on Rue Louis Vuitton.

> ## "
> # LV is for
> # LOUIS VUITTON,
> ## but it's also
> # FOR LOVERS:
> ## lovers of the moment,
> # LOVERS OF DETAIL,
> ## lovers of this time.
> ## "

PHARRELL WILLIAMS

ACKNOWLEDGEMENTS

To Jasmin Chua for our first biography together. Thank you for sharing my enthusiasm and diving into this book with such passion.

To Emily Hart for researching every detail of Louis Vuitton's life and discovering so many wonderful moments that make his journey unforgettable.

To Staci Barr for your enormous help with bringing all the pages together and sprinkling your touch of magic over everything.

To Martina Granolic for all the adventures that we have shared with our Louis Vuitton luggage. (If only our suitcases could talk!)

To Missy Lewis for your meticulous work and help among the illustrated pages.

To Murray Batten, thank you for creating such a handsome design to house Louis Vuitton's story.

To Todd Rechner for your incredible care and attention in seeing my books to their finished form. You've made each book something precious to hold, to read and to keep forever.

To my husband Craig and my children Gwyn and Will, thank you for listening to my endless anecdotes about Louis Vuitton and for being such great travel partners for all our family adventures!

ABOUT THE AUTHOR

Megan Hess was destined to draw. An initial career in graphic design evolved into art direction for some of the world's leading advertising agencies and for Liberty London. In 2008, Megan illustrated Candace Bushnell's number-one-bestselling book *Sex and the City*. This catapulted Megan onto the world stage, and she began illustrating portraits for *The New York Times*, *Vogue Italia*, *Vanity Fair* and *TIME*, that described Megan's work as 'love at first sight'.

Today, Megan is one of the world's most sought-after fashion illustrators, with a client list that includes Givenchy, Tiffany & Co., Valentino, Louis Vuitton and *Harper's Bazaar*. Megan's iconic style has been used in global campaigns for Fendi, Prada, Cartier, Dior and Salvatore Ferragamo. She has illustrated live for fashion shows such as Fendi at Milan Fashion Week, Chopard at the 2019 Cannes Film Festival, Viktor&Rolf and Christian Dior Couture.

Megan has created a signature look for Bergdorf Goodman, New York, and a bespoke bag collection for Harrods of London. She has illustrated a series of portraits for Michelle Obama, as well as portraits for Gwyneth Paltrow, Cate Blanchett and Nicole Kidman. She is also the Global Artist-in-Residence for the prestigious Oetker Hotel Collection.

Megan illustrates all her work with a custom Montblanc pen that she affectionately calls 'Monty'.

Megan has written and illustrated ten bestselling fashion books, as well as her much-loved series for children, *Claris the Chicest Mouse in Paris*.

When she's not in her studio working, you'll find her travelling around the world with her Louis Vuitton luggage.

_____

Visit Megan at meganhess.com

Published in 2025 by Hardie Grant Books, an imprint of Hardie Grant Publishing

Hardie Grant Books (Melbourne)
Wurundjeri Country
Level 11, 36 Wellington Street
Collingwood, Victoria 3066

Hardie Grant North America
2912 Telegraph Ave
Berkeley, California 94705

hardiegrant.com/books

Hardie Grant acknowledges the Traditional Owners of the country on which we work,
the Wurundjeri people of the Kulin nation and the Gadigal people of the Eora nation,
and recognises their continuing connection to the land, waters and culture.
We pay our respects to their Elders past and present.

A catalogue record for this
book is available from the
National Library of Australia

Louis Vuitton: The Illustrated World of a Fashion Icon
ISBN 978 1 76145 168 3
ISBN (ebook) 978 1 76144 3 138
10 9 8 7 6 5 4 3 2 1

Publisher: Jasmin Chua
Project Editor: Antonietta Anello
Researcher: Emily Hart
Creative Director: Kristin Thomas
Designer: Murray Batten
Head of Production: Todd Rechner
Production Controller: Jessica Harvie

Colour reproduction by Splitting Image Colour Studio
Printed in China by Leo Paper Products LTD.

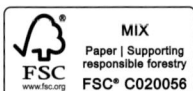

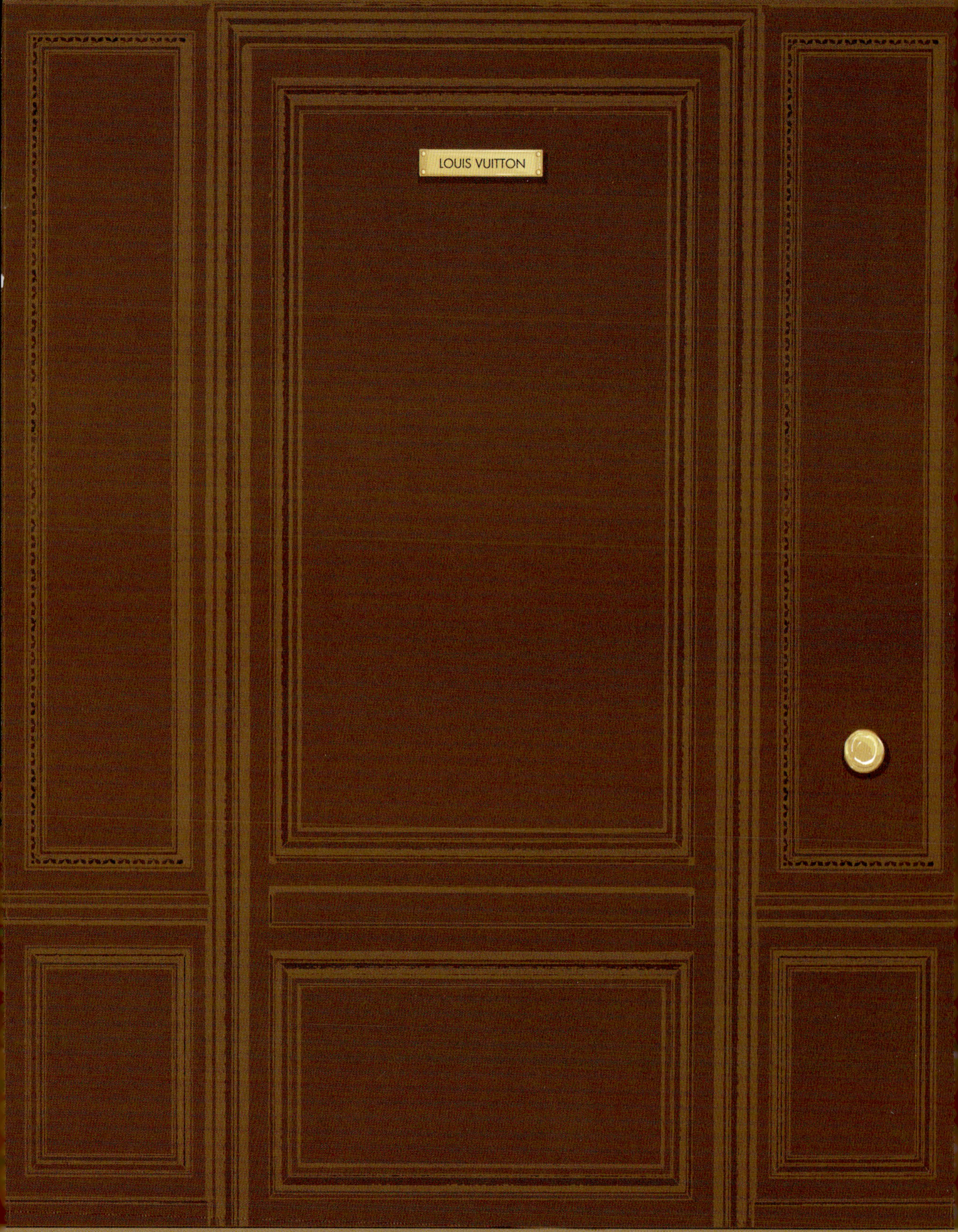
LOUIS VUITTON